GW00399908

A BOOT UP

PURBECK

Rodney Legg

First published in Great Britain in 2009

British Library Cataloguing-in-Publication Data
A CIP record for this title is available from the British Library

ISBN 978 1 906887 21 6

PiXZ Books
Halsgrove House, Ryelands Industrial Estate,
Bagley Road, Wellington, Somerset TA21 9PZ
Tel: 01823 653777
Fax: 01823 216796
email: sales@halsgrove.com

An imprint of Halstar Ltd, part of the Halsgrove group of companies
Information on all Halsgrove titles is available at: www.halsgrove.com

Printed and bound by Grafiche Flaminia, Italy

Contents

	How to use this book	4
1	Turners Puddle & Moreton	7
2	Corfe Castle & Chapman's Pool	13
3	East Chaldon & Durdle Door	19
4	Lulworth Cove & Mupe Bay	23
5	Tyneham & Worbarrow	29
6	Kimmeridge & Swyre Head	35
7	Worth Matravers & St Alban's Head	41
8	Durlston Head & Dancing Ledge	47
9	Ulwell & Godlingston	53
10	Ower & Studland	59

How to use this book

The Area

The Isle of Purbeck in Dorset is England in microcosm. Geology, which has thrown together several very different landscapes in the space of 70 square miles, provides the raw materials for a story that unfolds on the ground. Underneath, Mesozoic dinosaurs have left footsteps set in stone from the mud of warm lagoons, contemporary with the above-ground Fossil Forest. These are prize treasures of the Jurassic Coast. This was designated by Unesco in 2001 as the first natural World Heritage Site in Great Britain. It also boasts classic land-form features ranging from Durdle Door and Lulworth Cove to Old Harry Rocks and Studland's sands.

The stone is also key to the human story. The Normans used it for one of Europe's greatest castles, at Corfe, and went on to carve Purbeck marble for cathedrals and effigies across the land. Other strata have given us fossil fuel, with Britain's biggest on-shore oilfield stretching from Kimmeridge to Goathorn.

Superlatives are commonplace in Purbeck. It can claim some of the most varied and sunniest walking country in Britain. The weather claim is justified by a micro-climate caused by the other great lump of Dorset stone, in the shape of the Isle of Portland, which often deflects incoming weather fronts.

There is also more of Purbeck than there used to be. Historically the island - which in geographic terms it is not quite - ended on the landward side between Wareham and Lulworth. Since 1974, with the creation of Purbeck District Council, it has been stretched westwards to White Nothe and inland to Bere Regis.

Administrative changes are acknowledged here with walks that bring in delights from the outer parishes of Affpuddle, Chaldon Herring, Moreton, Turners Puddle and Wool. Literary associations abound from Thomas Hardy to Enid Blyton and meet the military in the form of Colonel T. E. Lawrence of Arabia and *The Seven Pillars of Wisdom*. The training ground for the world's first tanks reverberated to live-fire rehearsals for the D-Day landings. Purbeck is one of those rare places that is both addictive and quirky but never dull.

The Routes

All routes are circular - meaning they bring you back to the starting point - and are of moderate length. They vary from four to eleven miles and are graded from one to three boots - from easy to the more challenging. They are ideal for families or groups of friends looking for an afternoon in glorious historic countryside or for a more leisurely walk with a suitable pause at a pub or refreshment spot en route. None of the terrain is pushchair friendly, so backpack the toddler.

Starting points are given with map references and postcodes, because the latter are necessary for some car-borne navigation systems, including that used by an ambulance crew who told me they were 15 minutes late in arriving at an emergency because no postcode was given.

Direction details specify compass points which, clockwise, are N (north), NNE (north-northeast), E (east), ESE (east-southeast), SE (south-east), SSE (south-southeast), S (south), SSW (south-southwest), SW (south-west), WSW (west-southwest), W (west), WNW (west-northwest), NW (north-west) and WNW (west-northwest). The general direction can be assumed to remain the same until another compass point is given. Carry a compass.

Routes are along public rights of way or across access land. Both categories may be subject to change or diversion. Remember that conditions under foot will vary greatly according to the season and the weather. Do not set off along the cliffs if 'sea fret' - coastal fog - is likely.

Parking spaces are specified on the assumption that many walkers will arrive by car or bicycle. Where public transport is mentioned, there were options currently available, but check these with the provider before setting off and always make sure you also know the time of the last bus or train.

5

The Maps

Though we give a self-contained potted description of each walk you may need a map or global positioning system to find a parking point. Our sketch maps can only be a rough guide. A detailed map will prove useful if you stray from the route or are forced to cut the walk short. Remember that practical difficulties on the day may range from heat exhaustion to hill fog.

Conveniently, the area is currently covered by a single large-scale Ordnance Survey sheet which is Explorer Map OL15 (Purbeck & South Dorset). For availability access: www.ordnancesurvey.co.uk/leisure

Key to Symbols Used

Level of difficulty:

Easy 🦋

Fair 🦋 🦋

More challenging 🦋 🦋 🦋

Walk Locations

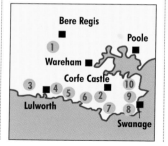

Map symbols:

🚗 Park & start

—— Tarred road

--- Unpaved road

----- Footpath

■ Building

+ Church

▲ Triangulation pillar or other landmark

🍺 Pub

🍴 Refreshments

🚻 WC

1 **Turners Puddle & Moreton**

An 8-mile sandy circuit through Lawrence of Arabia's rhododendrons

Level: 🐾
Length: 8 miles
Terrain: Easy-going, generally flat, along sandy heathland tracks.
Park & start: From the Forestry Commission car-park at **Culpepper's Dish** which is on the ridge above Briantspuddle, east of the B3390 a mile south of Affpuddle.
Start ref: SY 814 925.
Postcode: DT2 7HZ
Public transport: None.
Websites: www.lawrenceofarabia.co.uk
www.moretondorset.co.uk

Tanks have been synonymous with the heathland around Bovington Camp since their inception in 1916. It is also T. E. Lawrence's corner of Dorset's Hardy Country. To novelist Thomas Hardy it was his native heath. He visited the national hero in his Clouds Hill hideaway. En route we also pass the spot where Lawrence was fatally injured in a motor-cycle crash, visit his funeral church at Moreton, and see his nearby grave. Two rivers - the Piddle and the Frome - flow through tranquil water-meadows. The walk also brings in Briantspuddle and virtually deserted Turners Puddle. Wildlife ranges from herons in the ditches, buzzards in the sky, and deer and nightjars on the ground.

1 Set off by walking back to the car-park entrance, in order to glimpse Culpepper's Dish, a massive swallow hole shrouded in shrub on the opposite side of the carriageway, resulting from the dynamic geology of these parts when its sands and gravels were inundated. Turn left (W) along the road for 100 metres.

2 Turn right (N) into the trees for 225 metres. Turn right (NE) at the junction of tracks and stay on the main path. Descend to the cottages of **Briantspuddle** hamlet in 500 metres.

3 Turn left (N) along the tarred road and proceed straight ahead at the cross-roads in 250 metres. Cross the Georgian bridge

Culpepper's Dish.

over the **River Piddle** in 150 metres. Continue for a further 350 metres.

4 Turn right (E) into a farm track, with fields to the left and riverside scrub on the right, to **Turners Puddle** in 1,300 metres. Pass **Holy Trinity Church** and the farmhouse home of Sir Gilbert and Lady Violet Debenham.

5 Turn right (S) along a gravel road which fords a stream and then crosses the main channel of the River Piddle in 200 metres. This is a public road with footbridges for pedestrians. Beyond the river, in 350 metres we emerge in **Throop** hamlet.

6 Turn left along the road, up through **Throop Hollow**, to **Throop Clump** cross-roads in 800 metres. Continue straight across. There is a Bronze Age burial mound under the trees to the right. In a further 800 metres we come to a road junction at **Dead Woman's Stone**. The stone, which marked a suicide burial, was removed by desert hero Colonel Thomas Edward Lawrence and sculptor Eric Kennington and now lies in a garden in Briantspuddle.

Briantspuddle Bridge

gamekeeper's cottage, which was his home from 1923 (and is opened to the public by the National Trust).

 8 Turn left (E) up the road towards Bere Regis. Then turn right (S) in 100 metres. Follow the boundary of the **Tank Training**

Area for 800 metres to a commemorative stone and oak tree marking the spot where Lawrence was fatally injured in a motor-cycle accident in 1935.

9 Cross the road to the gates of **Training Area W1**. Go

7 Bear left (SE), through a bridleway gate, into a triangle of heathland which has been restored by Dorset County Council. Cross this vestige of **Tonerspuddle Heath** and keep the fence of the military training area to your left. Emerge from the rhododendron bushes at a junction in 750 metres. Those on the other side were planted to hide **Lawrence of Arabia's Cottage** at **Clouds Hill**, an 1806-built

Throop

Lawrence of Arabia's Cottage

over the stile immediately to the right of the gates and warning notices. Follow the fence straight ahead (SW) with tank tracks to the left and pine trees to the right. Bear right in 700 metres, into **Moreton Plantation**, and descend to a track in 400 metres. Turn left (S) along it, down to the next path junction in another 400 metres.

10 Turn right (W), across a tree-less bog, and pass **The Glade** in 400 metres. Note the complex series of bridges and former water-courses beyond it. Walk beside these to the junction with the track from Snelling Farm in 300 metres.

11 Turn right (NW) to sandy **Moreton Drive** in 350 metres. Turn left (SW) to the fields and water-meadows beside the **River**

Briantspuddle and adjacent Bladen Valley were turned into a model agricultural community by London department store owner Ernest Debenham between 1919 and 1928.

Frome. Bear right along the main track in 200 metres. This is a public road which brings us to **Longbridge** and the widest ford in Dorset in 350 metres. To the right there is a wartime pillbox, built in 1940, concealed in the scrub.

12 Cross the bridge into Moreton for triple diversions. **St Nicholas Church** is to the left at the second road junction. T. E. Lawrence's grave is around the corner in the **Cemetery** which is reached by going straight ahead at the third junction. The **Old School** is a bistro and tea-rooms.

13 For our onward route, return across the Longbridge and follow the road to the lesser bridge in 350 metres, at the bottom end of Moreton Drive. Turn left (N) across a stile beside a gate and enter the field. Bear right across the pasture, keeping the scrubby wood and its fence to your right, and cross a series of stiles across the fields to the footbridge into Moreton Plantation in 600 metres.

(14) Proceed straight ahead, through rhododendrons and conifers to the junction with the main woodland track in 600 metres. This spot is known as **Spyway** though its cottage has gone. Turn left and then bear right through the laurels. There are fields to the left as we approach the road in 400 metres.

(15) Cross to the forest road (NE) on the other side. This passes **Okers Wood House** in 500 metres. In a further 600 metres we go under the 400 kilowatt wires of the National Grid strung between 160-feet pylons. Then in 200 metres the track passes to the left of **Rimsmoor Pond**. This sphagnum sponge in a heathland hollow features in Thomas Hardy's *The Return of the Native* (when Mrs Yeobright asks a boy if it has dried up). After the 'bottomless' pond, in 100 metres, we come to a cross-roads of forest tracks. Do not take any of the gravel tracks but instead go straight ahead (N), up the lesser path between the pines, to pass to the left of a Bronze Age round barrow on the hilltop in 350 metres. Then turn right along the roadside fire-break to return to the car-park in 75 metres.

Longbridge

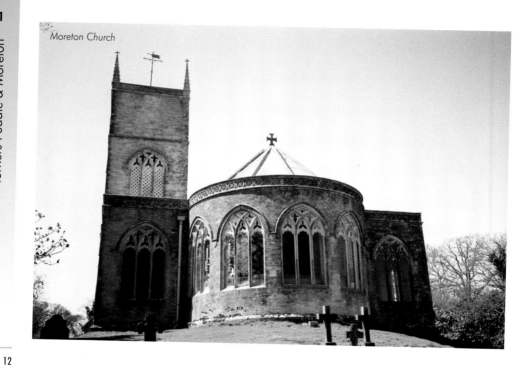

Moreton Church

2 Corfe Castle & Chapman's Pool

Eight miles between Corfe Castle, Kingston & the English Channel

This is Dorset's great mediaeval landscape. Dominated by Corfe Castle, it includes contemporary pastures on Corfe Common, with sledge-tracks slashed into its ridge to show where blocks of Purbeck marble were hauled across it and down to village workshops. Stone for effigies and cathedrals was exported via Ower Quay in Poole Harbour where incoming shipments included timber for building the royal fortress.

A renaissance in carving and the stone trade is represented by Kingston's outsized church, in Victorian Gothic, by architect George Edmund Street for the 2nd Earl of Eldon. Seawards, beyond

Level: 🐾 🐾
Length: 8 miles
Terrain: Variable, across the spring-line in places, with minor slopes.
Park & start: From the National Trust's **Castle View** car-park, beside the Visitor Centre below Corfe Castle, or around the corner in the long layby beside the road signed to Church Knowle.
Start ref: SY 959 824.
Postcode: BA20 5ED
Public transport: Buses and trains between Wareham and Swanage.
Websites: www.corfe-castle.co.uk
www.ukfossils.co.uk

Encombe, the walk reaches Chapman's Pool and overlooks St Alban's Head.

Corfe Castle

1 Set off towards Church Knowle from **St Edward's Bridge** (SW) with the **Castle Hill** to the left and **Corfe River** to your right. Cross the next bridge, opposite the site of **West Mill**, in 250 metres. Pass the entrance to **Vineyard Farm** and thatched **Vineyard Cottage** in 50 metres and proceed uphill for a further 80 metres.

2 Turn left into the field beside **The Rings** siege-work. These date from King Stephen's spat with the barons and were re-used by Cromwellian forces in the Civil War. Continue straight ahead from the road-side gate (SE), over the stile and across the field. Head towards the right-hand side of Corfe Castle village and cross a stile into the meadow. Cross the river

at the footbridge in 300 metres.

3 Bear right (SW) on the other side to join another path along the other side of the field in 100 metres. Go through the kissing gate beneath the offshoot power cables in 150 metres. Enter **Corfe Common** - also National Trust owned - and descend to the **Copper Bridge** in 50 metres. This is a single arch of stone, with a passage 6 feet wide between parapets, just wide enough for a cart.

Copper Bridge

4 Having re-crossed the river there are three path options in the arable field. The fence crosses the site of **Bucknowle Roman Villa**. Our path bears left (S), following the hedgerow, to fence bars in 250 metres. Enter this meadow and turn right, across the stile beyond the power pole in 150 metres. Here a footbridge takes us across the river again.

5 Head uphill (SW) through the scrub and across the field, towards a stile in the hedgerow on the

Corfe Castle is on the site of the Anglo-Saxon royal 'domus' where boy-king Edward the Martyr was assassinated in 978 by members of his stepmother's household.

far side in 400 metres. Instead of crossing this, however, we stop and look back at the classic view of Corfe Castle in the gap in the Purbeck Hills. Now turn left (E) on another public path, down to a gate in the corner of the field in 200 metres. Turn left, up a farm track, to the junction in 75 metres.

6 Turn right (S) along the farm road, passing a Mesolithic site in the dip, and climb to **Blashenwell Farm** in 600 metres. Turn right at the farm and follow a bridleway which bends towards the slope uphill into the right-hand corner of the woods in 600 metres. Go through the gate into the conifers. Continue straight ahead (SE) at the woodland cross-roads in 200 metres. Then pass the garages

to the road in Kingston hamlet in 100 metres (divert down the road to see the cathedral-size Victorian church and visit the Scott Arms).

7 Turn right (W) for our onward route, for 100 metres, and then fork left (SW) into the central of three options. Despite 'Private Property' notices this is a public footpath to Houns-tout and the coast. Continue almost straight ahead at a complicated six-way junction of tracks in 400 metres. Our path is the second turning on the left. It is signed for **Hill View** which we pass, to our left, and at the end of **Quarry Wood** in 300 metres we are treated to a glorious view of the **Golden Bowl**, below the obelisk to the right. Encombe House is its centrepiece.

(**8**) Follow the stone wall (S) to the coast path on **Houns-tout Cliff** in 1,500 metres. Freshwater, Kimmeridge Bay, Bindon Hill and Portland are to the right. We turn left (E), towards St Alban's Head,

with the English Channel down to the right. Descend the steps and slope to a stile above **Chapman's Pool** in 400 metres.

(**9**) Turn left (N) in the field towards Westhill Cottage. Turn right in 300 metres across a culvert above the scrubby gully. Turn right along the tarred road and then fork left (NE) at its cul-de-sac in 125 metres. Pass between the cottages of **Hill Bottom** in 800 metres. Turn right along the road, beside **Hill Bottom Cottage**, and follow it around to the left at the next set of path junctions in 75 metres.

(**10**) Turn left in 100 metres, below Renscombe Farm, on to a public path which follows the

Encombe stile

upper course of the stream, up a deep-cut valley for 700 metres. The bridleway then turns left (N) to skirt the side of **Swanworth Quarry**. In 500 metres we approach farm buildings and turn left and then immediately right (NE) through the gate out of the field, which has an 8-feet high Bronze Age burial mound. **Afflington Barrow** was opened by Victorian antiquary John Austen, to reveal a primary 'Beaker' cremation and rows of skeletons which had been inserted later. The final 350 metres to **Afflington Barn** buildings are between double hedgerows.

(11) Cross the main road (N) to the double-hedged track on the other side. Go through a gate In 200 metres and bear left (NW) to head down the slope between clumps of blackthorn and gorse. Follow the Purbeck Way towards a very visible Corfe Castle. Towards the bottom of the slope, in 600 metres, the main track bends to the right. Here we leave it, by turning left, and exit from the corner of the scrubby limestone downland.

(12) Follow the edge of the field beside the lush wooded gully.

Beyond it is the ostrich country of Scoles Farm. Bear left into the field on approaching Corfe Common in 700 metres and cross the footbridge to the left of **Lower Lynch Cottage**. Turn right in the field and follow the fence down to the scrub immediately beyond the drive in 100 metres. A path through the bushes leads down to a stile in 50 metres where we re-enter National Trust land.

(13) Cross the stream and continue straight ahead on to the barrow-studded ridge in 350 metres. Turn left (W) and follow the line of Bronze Age burial mounds for 300 metres. Cross the road below and to the right of the brow of the hill. Beware of fast cars. Re-enter **Corfe Common** on the other side, passing National Trust signs, and proceed straight ahead, keeping to the left of

Houns-tout view

the signed path - between it and the continuing line of barrows along the ridge - to the unfenced road across the common in about 750 metres.

14 Turn right (N) along it, for some 350 metres, to the cattle-grid and turning circle. Continue straight ahead, into what is now **West Street** and passes through the heart of old Corfe to the **Fox Inn** and the **Town Hall** (claiming to be England's oldest) in 800 metres.

15 Proceed straight ahead, in 50 metres, beside the 1897-dated monument for Queen Victoria's diamond jubilee on the ancient **Market Cross**. Carry on towards **Corfe Castle**. Buy a ticket or flash your National Trust card for our last optional diversion.

Swanworth Quarry

16 Either way we proceed along a public path which crosses the four-arch cobbled bridge and then turns immediately right on the other side, between the moat and the right-hand tower of the Gatehouse. The path passes above the Trust's Boar Mill and becomes a sloping terrace down to a gate in 300 metres beside the turnpike milestone ('IV miles from Wareham'). Your car is across the road.

In continuous use from 65 to 375 AD, Bucknowle Roman villa and workshops were discovered in 1975 by Tony Brown from Corfe Castle - who found pottery and masonry in molehills - and excavations from 1976 to 1991 uncovered a deluxe glass jug from Rhineland.

3 **East Chaldon & Durdle Door**

A 9-mile circuit that explores the cliffs and downland between Lulworth and Ringstead

The heart of the Jurassic Coast, with classic landform geology from the great uplift caused by the African tectonic plate colliding with that of Eurasia, at a time when our global position was much closer to the tropics. The chalk deposits comprise billions of microscopic fossils from an earlier era of warm seas.

These are the white cliffs of Dorset, with a detached chalk stack at Butter Rock, and outer ragged ribbons of projecting limestone. It is a landscape redolent with literary associations, including inevitable Hardy connections, plus a pot pourri of very different creative minds

Level: ♥ ♥ ♥
Length: 9 miles
Terrain: Serious descents and ascents, from sea-level to 500 feet, but on mainly firm, well-trod paths.
Park and start: At **East Chaldon** in the vicinity of the village green.
Start ref: SY 791 833.
Postcode: DT2 8DN
Public transport: Buses from Wareham and Wool, but join en route via Lulworth.
Websites: www.lulworthonline.co.uk
www.weymouth-dorset.co.uk

and lives. They range from pioneer writer David Garnett and the diverse Powys brothers to lesbian lovers Valentine Ackland and Sylvia Townsend Warner, and the promiscuously heterosexual Bertrand Russell.

Map labels

Owermoigne Down
10
11 Five Marys ✱✱
12
Lord's Barrow ✱
13
Sailor's Return
9
North Holworth Farm
1
2
East Chaldon
Sea Barn
Holworth House
3
Sleight Buildings
Daggers Gate
Whitenothe Cottages
▲ Navigation markers
Newlands Farm
4
...ad
7
Caravan Camp
...tional Trust Undercliff
White Nothe
Fountain Rock
6
Bat's Head
5
Durdle Door
Man o' War Cove

500 m

Man o' War Cove

Set off along the lane towards Winfrith Newburgh (E) and approach the village sign from the rear in 600 metres.

Turn right (S) up a stony track and pass a bungalow in 50 metres. Continue along the track around two corners and into a dry chalkland combe. Fork left in 500 metres, following the main track up the valley, and go through a gate in 75 metres. In 250 metres we go through another gate, along a grassy path on the left-hand side of the hedge. For the next 200 metres the farm track remains parallel to us, on the other side, and then our path enters the next valley.

Climb up a chalky track to **Sleight Buildings** in 800 metres. Here our onward track turns left (SE) to barns at **Daggers Gate** in 700 metres. Turn right, up the road, to the bend and house on the corner in 350 metres.

Turn right (S), via **Newlands Farm** and the caravan camp, to the downland slope overlooking **St Oswald's Bay** and **Man o' War Cove** in 800 metres. This offshore ribbon of rocks was notorious for shipwrecks.

Turn right (W) along the coast path. In 400 metres we pass the projecting limestone rock-arch of **Durdle Door**, to a skyline backdrop of the English Channel and Portland,

almost detached from the white chalk cliffs. Next, in 400 metres, we drop almost to sea-level at **Scratchy Bottom** and then climb the next wave of chalkland up and over **Swyre Head**. Offshore are a series of lime-stone rocks from the Bull and Blind Cow to the Cow and Calf, with the inshore Butter Rock being a chalk stack in 600 metres.

6 Here we pass **Bat's Head** peninsula which is perforated by the natural arch of Bat's Hole. In 1,500 metres, after the slopes of **The Warren** and **Middle Bottom**, we pass navigation markers in **West Bottom** which were provided for mariners to line up behind them, to guarantee the safe deep-water passage into Portland Harbour. A column of cliffside chalk is known as Fountain Rock (among a series of coastal fea-tures yet to be given their names by the Ordnance Survey).

7 In 1,000 metres we pass **Whitenothe Cottages**, built by the Coast Guard service, which at 495 feet above sea level plus 30 feet of western elevation are the highest buildings on the Dorset coast. Beyond, in National Trust land, follow the clifftop path (NW) to a stile in 750 metres. Continue straight ahead across the coastal downland, between the wood on the **Burning Cliff** and the hilltop house.

8 Beyond, in 600 metres, we cross a stile in the corner of the pasture and join the gravel track. Follow it straight ahead for 75 metres and then turn right (N) inland. The track becomes a concrete farm road and then a tarred public highway on passing through the gates at **North Holworth Farm** in 1,500 metres. Banks and closes of the mediaeval lost village of **Holworth** lie in the field to the right.

Durdle Door

9 Continue straight ahead, passing the pond, up and over the hill, for 750 metres. Just over the brow - where a Bronze Age round barrow is scrub-covered to the left on **Owermoigne Down**, we turn right (E). Go through the left-hand of the two gates (ignoring a single gate to the right).

10 Then follow the hawthorn hedgerow straight ahead, along the ridge, with a wide view of the Frome valley to the left. Go through double gates at the end of the field in 600 metres. Follow the hedgerow for the length of the next two fields to a concrete emplacement and **Lord's Barrow** in 800 metres.

11 Cross the road to a bridleway gate on the other side and follow the fence for 1,000 metres. Proceed straight ahead across the next road, for 50 metres, and then fork left along the ridgeway which passes the **Five Marys** barrow group. There are six mounds, actually, with the 'Mary' name being a corruption for the Old English word 'mere' for a boundary.

12 In 300 metres we reach a fence and turn right (SW). Follow the path downhill into the scrub in 150 metres. In a further 50 metres we emerge on the tarred road.

13 Turn left (S) to return to East Chaldon via the **Sailor's Return** in 800 metres. This is where David Garnett set his novel of that name in 1925. It was an English literary rarity, in featuring a black heroine, not that she made it on to the inn sign. Beyond, in 150 metres, is the village green.

4 **Lulworth Cove & Mupe Bay**

Venturing into the Lulworth Ranges for a 4-mile round-walk plus an extra mile of enticing diversions

Level: 🐾 🐾
Length: 4 miles
Terrain: Firm chalkland paths with a couple of stiff slopes.
Park and start: In the car-park at **Lulworth Cove** at the end of the B3070 from Wareham and B3071 from Wool.
Start ref: SY 822 811.
Postcode: BH20 5RQ
Public transport: Buses from Wareham and Wool.
Websites: www.jurassiccoast.com
www.lulworth.com

This walk is only available when the Lulworth Range Walks are open. That should be the case most weekends and during the Christmas, Easter and August block-leave periods. Check the signs as you approach the area from Wareham, Wool or Winfrith or in advance with the Range Office on 01-929 404 700. Once you are inside the ranges for Armoured Fighting Vehicles stay within designated safe zones (marked by yellow posts) and resist the temptation to stray or remove or touch any item or piece of metal or plastics. These are live-firing areas, used intensively for gunnery practice by armoured cars, helicopters and tanks, so there will inevitably be unexploded missiles and shells lurking in the great expanses of long grass. Hands off the boy-toys.

West Lulworth

School
Bindon Hill
Cockpit Head
Cove Inn
ARMY RANGES
Mupe Bay
Mupe Rocks
Lulworth Cove
Pepler's Point
Fossil Forest
Smugglers' Cave

2
3
6
1
4
5
13
7
14
11
12
10
9
8

↑ Worth

500 m

1 Set off by returning to the main road and turn left (N), crossing it, to the raised section of old road beside **Cromwell House Hotel**.

2 Turn right (E) in 500 metres, beside **Cove House**, up **Bindon Road**. Turn left (N), into **Sunnyside Terrace**, in 50 metres. Proceed to the end of it in 200 metres. Fork right here (NE), along the path above **Limberlost**, and also bear right - down the steps - after the house, in 75 metres. Keep to this narrow, double-hedged track, with gardens and paddocks down to the left.

3 In 500 metres we cross a stile and enter the pasture above the school. Turn right (S) and follow

the hedgerow to a stile in 200 metres to the right of Danger Flag No. 5. Beyond it, walk up through the scrub to the ditch and bank of **Bindon Hill** Iron Age fort, with the perimeter fence of the Lulworth Ranges to the left.

Paths open

4 Turn left in 150 metres, at red flag No. 4, through the **Radar Entrance** of the Lulworth Range Walks provided it is open. If it is locked you will have to return to Lulworth Cove by continuing over the hill and turning right along the coastal path.

Cockpit Head

5 Our onward route (E), if access is available, is across the top of Bindon Hill with the ancient earthwork and its star-sign indicators to the left. Fork left after the **Radar Station** in 200 metres. Walk a chalky length of prehistoric ridgeway with 20th-century military banks either side of it. Proceed above the bearing pickets from **B8** to **B5**. These are for directing tank gunnery by the Royal Armoured Corps,

on **Bindon Range** down to the left, towards a series of rail-mounted moving targets emplaced below the slope. Ensure that here and elsewhere you keep to the strip of safe ground between yellow-painted marker posts. Proceed straight ahead to the mast beside red flag No. 9 in 900 metres. In a further 100 metres we pass the pyramidal monument to soldiers whose ashes have been scattered in this area. Next are Bronze Age burial mounds.

6 Continue to the stile and gate above bearing picket **B7** in 250 metres and then for a further 75 metres towards the great seascape of Worbarrow Tout and St Alban's Head. Approach **Cockpit Head**. Seawards there is a breath-taking view to a salient of rocks jutting

out into Worbarrow Bay. Lulworth Camp and Lulworth Castle dominate the inland plain.

7 Turn right (SW) and zig-zag down the steep slope to **Mupe Bay** in 500 metres. This is prime butterfly-rich chalkland turf, south-facing and never sprayed with chemicals, which can become surprisingly warm when it is in the lee of the wind. Descend into scrubby land-

> *Originally palisaded, the bank and ditch across Bindon Hill was one of the first on the South Coast to be built by Celtic immigrants from the continent, to protect their settlement prior to 500 BC.*

Mupe Rocks

slipped terrain on pockets of multi-coloured Wealden sands and clays.

(8) Here you have an optional diversion. Descend the staggered series of steps to the stony beach and **Mupe Rocks**. If you

follow the shore around to the right for as far as you can safely go, you reach the **Smugglers' Cave** hidden in the corner in 500 metres.

(9) Having returned to the top of the landslipped slopes, continue

along the cliff path (W) to the ruins of the winch-house that was used to raise kegs from the cave in 400 metres. Also pass the moulded concrete of a 1940 anti-invasion pillbox that was shuttered with corrugated iron.
In 900 metres we reach the range boundary fence above a long rocky platform above the waves.

(10) Turn left down the steps (S) for a well worthwhile 300 metre excursion (E) along the inward

Fossil Forest

lip of low but precipitous cliffs. This is studded with the cycad stumps of the **Fossil Forest** which is the greatest single treasure of Dorset's internationally-famed Jurassic Coast.

 Return to the gate at the top beneath danger flag No. 1 for a second optional diversion along the cliff path (W) for 300 metres to **Pepler's Point**.

 Our onward and outward route turns inland (N) on the Army's side of the chain-link fence, down to the gate and stile beside red flag No. 2 in 250 metres. Go through the gate and leave the Lulworth Ranges beside the grassy original site of **Bindon Abbey**. Pass the quaint half-chapel **Little Bindon Cottage**.

 Take a tide and weather check. Head towards **Lulworth Cove** (E) and walk its shoreline around to the boathouses and cafe, in 750 metres, if it is safe to do so. If not - should waves be breaking against or near the cliffs - you must take the cliff path (N) up and over the western end of Bindon Hill.

 Either way we find ourselves in the cul-de-sac street that passes the former **Coastguard Station**, **Mill House Hotel** and exquisite miniature **Dolls' House** cottage to **Cove Inn** and the cafe beside the car-park in 400 metres.

Pepler's Point

Inner Cove

5 **Tyneham & Worbarrow**

Military ecology with an evocative 4-mile circuit of ruined cottages and breathtaking cliffs

This is Dorset's biggest natural wildness. The ghost village of Tyneham and its spectacular coastline are only accessible when the Lulworth Range Walks are open. This is generally the case at weekends, Easter, Christmas and through the block-leave month of August. Check on boards or with the Range Office on 01-929 404 700. These are ranges for

Armoured Fighting Vehicles, though usually on the lighter side in Tyneham Valley, as battle-tanks stay on the other side of the hill. Tyneham also serves as an overshoot area for tank rounds that land in the sea. Great quantities of munitions have been used here since before D-Day, so don't stray and don't touch warnings apply. The coast equals that of

Level: 🥾 🥾 🥾
Length: 4 miles
Terrain: Much long grass with a demanding climb up the escarpment from sea-level to 550 feet.
Park and start: In the car-park at **Tyneham** village, reached by turning off the hilltop road between East Lulworth and Creech Hill, to the south of Wareham.
Start ref: SY 882 802.
Postcode: BH20 5DF (for Creech Hill)
Public transport: None.
Websites: www.dorsetcoast.com
www.mod.gov.uk

Lulworth in its beauty and variety. A savannah-like expanse of grassy slopes rises into a ribbon of limestone crags along the wedge-shaped line of Gad Cliff.

Whiteway Hill ⑦
Rook Grove
Flower's Barrow ⑥
⑤
ARMY RANGES
⑧ **Tyneham**
④
Arish Mell
Worbarrow Bay
The Gwyle
① 🚗 Tyneham Farm ■
③ Gold Down
Worbarrow Tout
Pondfield Cove
Gad Cliff ②
Brandy Bay

Set off (S) through the gate 250 metres beyond the village, and cross the **Gwyle Stream** to the corner beside **Tyneham Farm** in 75 metres. Leave the main track and continue straight ahead, across the stile beside a cattle-grid, and then fork left (SE) in 10 metres. Cross the pasture, between yellow marker posts, and climb the slope for 250 metres. Here the track bears right (SW) up the incline to a stile and the coastal path on **Gad Cliff** in 300 metres, above bearing pickets **T7** and **T8**.

② Turn right (W) along the inner edge of the limestone crags above **Brandy Bay** and its wild undercliff. Head towards Portland and the white cliffs of Arish Mell, Cockpit Head and Bindon Hill. In 1,000 metres the path descends **Gold Down** to **Pondfield Cove** and **Worbarrow Tout** in 500 metres (offering an optional diversion up to the left, to bearing picket **T3** which is a stiff 150 metres away on the summit).

③ Cross the beach and the outlet of the Gwyle Stream to the left of the stone and grass platform marking the site of fisherman Jack Miller's **Sea Cottage**. In 50 metres the onward path crosses a footbridge and then passes through yellow posts in the fence-line in 15 metres. Note, as geographer Anne Jones pointed out to me, how the wind has shaped waves in the blackthorn bushes.

④ The upward course (N) passes the sites of Sheepleaze,

Walk between the yellow posts

Tyneham Village

which was the Draper family's holiday home, and the Bungalow in 150 metres. The path becomes increasingly steep for the next 1,000 metres. Cross a stile near the summit into the banks and ditches defending **Flower's Barrow** hill-fort.

 For an optional diversion, this time expending little energy, proceed through the Iron Age earthworks for stunning views seawards to Arish Mell and inland to Monastery Farm - named for Trappist monks given refuge by the Catholic Welds after the French Revolution - and family's home at Lulworth Castle. Turn around in 400 metres.

6 Our onward route is the other way (E), on the **Ridgeway**

Tyneham Church

from the outer banks and ditches along the main line of the Purbeck Hills. A military road rises from the left in 700 metres, after bearing picket **H7**, and we continue straight ahead (NE) along the hilltop. Pass an Ordnance Survey triangulation pillar on **Whiteway Hill** in 500 metres.

From here the hilltop track drops into a dip, at red flag **No. 21**, in a further 500 metres.

7 Turn sharp right (SW) on to a flinty road down the hillside. This heads towards Worbarrow Tout. Rook Grove is the wood to the left.

Though Tyneham parishioners were promised they could return home when the conflict was over, the pledge was overtaken by events, as the Attlee Government deemed the area vital for military training during the new Cold War.

Faint lines beside it show the cultivation strips of a mediaeval open field. The untarred road bends to the left (S) beside it, in 400 metres, at the bottom of the incline.

8 Proceed for 500 metres to enter the ruins of **Tyneham Village** to the right of **St Mary's Church**. Start by bearing right (W)

to see the little lakes, lovingly recreated by Major Mick Burgess, and the **Rectory** with its cobbled self-draining courtyard. Then head through the trees (S) to the Taylor family's **Laundry Cottages** and **Grant and Wellman Cottages** beyond. Turn left (E) to **Shepherd's Cottage** at the south end of **Post Office Row**. In the centre were the Driscolls, at the Post Office, followed by the **Post Office**. Beside the former front garden is a restored vintage concrete telephone box, model K1 mark 236, installed in 1929. Next, after the Pritchards' end cottage, are the intact **School** museum and ruins of Rectory Cottages. Almost lastly, and definitely not least, is **St Mary's Church** with its memorials to the ruling Williams and Bond families

Flower's Barrow

who lived in Tyneham House - out-of-bounds up the valley - for half a millennium. **Gardener's Cottage** beyond was home of the Gould family.

Worbarrow Bay

6 **Kimmeridge & Swyre Head**

A 5.5-mile round-walk at Kimmeridge contrasts Purbeck's highest point with undersea wildlife

Level: 🥾 🥾
Length: 5.5 miles
Terrain: Clearly marked tracks with a couple of climbs.
Park and start: In the old quarry at the top of **Kimmeridge Hill**, 30 metres from the hilltop junction above Kimmeridge, where roads come up the valley from Church Knowle and Steeple.
Start ref: SY 918 800.
Postcode: BH20 5PE
Public transport: None.
Websites: www.dorsetforyou.com
www.maps.google.co.uk

Kimmeridge is a neat stone and thatched village of two short streets at the foot of a limestone escarpment. This rises into barrow-topped

Swyre Head which at 666 feet above sea-level is the highest point in the Isle of Purbeck. A mile away, southwards, is the austere shoreline of relatively low, grey, oily cliffs that are the backdrop to Kimmeridge Bay. Visually, this is a rough and friable grandeur, contrasting with clean-cut rocky cliffs around each corner, perfumed with a sulphurous whiff of oil and kelp that may well evoke early memories of the seaside. Shale-

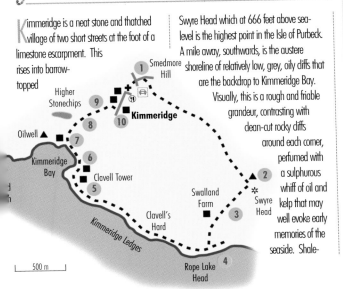

Higher Stonechips
Smedmore Hill
Kimmeridge
Oilwell
Kimmeridge Bay
Clavell Tower
Clavell's Hard
Kimmeridge Ledges
Swalland Farm
Swyre Head
Rope Lake Head

500 m

based industries have operated since the Iron Age, for mineral products as varied as alum, benzene, gas, glass, sanitary carbon and crude oil. Dorset Wildlife Trust now manages the bay as a marine nature reserve.

Swyre Head

1 Set off back to the junction and then turn right (NE) towards Church Knowle and Corfe Castle. Walk along the road for 75 metres and then turn right (SE) up a stony track, through a gate, to follow the stone wall at the edge of the ridge overlooking the coastal flatlands around Smedmore House. In 2,000 metres this brings us to a Bronze Age round barrow at the top of **Swyre Head** which at 666 feet above sea level is the highest point in the Isle of Purbeck.

Clavell Tower lookout was built as a folly in 1831 by Revd John Richards who adopted the Clavell name after inheriting the family's Smedmore House estate.

2 On passing the Ordnance Survey pillar our onward route turns sharply right (SW) across a stile. Follow pointers downhill to the 'Coast path'. This link is a permissive path, though hopefully for the long term, as it is also used for a Dorset County Council round-walk: 'The path beyond this point is not a public right of way but the owner allows the public to use it for the time being.'

3 Descend the escarpment in a more or less straight line towards the sea. There is a stile at the end of the field and another sign-post after a length of dirt track to the cliffs at **Rope Lake Head** in 1,500 metres.

4 Turn right (NW) on joining the coastal path. This overlooks the Kimmeridge Ledges which have

Kimmeridge Bay

claimed innumerable shipwrecks. In 1,000 metres, at the second of three footbridges across small streams at **Clavell's Hard**, we pass above traces of Victorian shale workings. As well as mine opening - not accessible - there is also an area which self-combusted and burnt for several months in 1973. These days all you are likely to experience is the distinctive Kimmeridge smell from the blackstone ledges of grey bituminous shales which jut out into the sea.

 The next notable feature is the colonnaded **Clavell Tower** in 2,000 metres. This is back on the skyline after having been moved a short distance inland in 2008. It was dismantled by the Landmark Trust and rebuilt to save it from falling down the cliff.

 Follow the path down through the scrub to Dorset Wildlife Trust's marine nature reserve in **Kimmeridge Bay** in 250 metres. Life underwater can be experienced in real-time thanks to video surveillance.

Kimmeridge Post Office

Rope Lake Head

 Our onward path is the cliffside option to the left of the access road and then the car-park. Head for the former Coast Guard Cottages at **Gaulter Gap** in 400 metres.

 Bear right (N) for 100 metres, inland to the access road to the BP's oilfield, which dates from 1959. Follow this leftwards for about

The treacherous Kimmeridge Ledges were notorious for shipwrecks, being second only to the infamous Chesil Beach, with records stretching back to the plundering of the stricken ship Welfare in 1371 - valued at £2,000 which was then a colossal sum.

100 metres, to the bridge, and then turn right (NE) along a path which follows the stream to **Kimmeridge** village. Take the right-hand option in the field after **Higher Stonechips** wood in 250 metres.

 Turn right in next arable field as well, and continue to

follow the stream to the gardens, in 750 metres. Turn right (E) to cross the stream to the street, opposite **Stonefield**, in 150 metres.

 Turn left (NE), uphill beside the thatched cottages, to the **Post Office Tea-room** and **St Michael's Church** in 400 metres.

39

Proceed straight ahead from the churchyard steps - along the path to the right of the graves - and then directly up the escarpment to return to the junction beside the quarry car-park in 250 metres.

Kimmeridge sunset

Clavell Tower

Sulphur-smelling blackstone shale rock from Kimmeridge was mined in the Victorian period and shipped to Weymouth, for the extraction of gas (11,300 cubic feet per ton) which was used for street lighting in Wareham and Paris.

7 Worth Matravers & St Alban's Head

Stunning scenery all the way in a 6-mile coastal circuit of the southern quarries and cliffs

Level: 🥾🥾
Length: 6 miles
Terrain: Agricultural coastline, with arable fields rather than access land, but retaining its rougher edges and slopes.
Park and start: In the village car-park beside the road into **Worth Matravers** from the B3069 east of Kingston.
Start ref: SY 974 777.
Postcode: BH19 3LF
Public transport: Buses from Corfe Castle and Swanage.
Websites: www.beerintheevening.com
www.worldheritage.net

Intimate views are dominated by stone. Stone cottages, stone quarries, and the stone plateau generally. Its iconic piece of indigenous art, a stone pillar on a ledge 350 feet above the race at St Alban's Head, was left in situ by quarrymen as a seamark. The distant view is across to more stone on Portland. In between are grey shale cliffs beyond Chapman's Pool and treacherous ledges that have claimed a multitude of shipwrecks. The Square and Compass in Worth Matravers is named for the symbolic tools of the Masonic trade. The Norman 'Capella Sancti Aldhelmi', on the southern tip of the Isle of Purbeck, was named for the Anglo-Saxon saint who was bishop of Sherborne from 705 to his death in

709. On the other hand, mariners and Dorset countrymen always have called it St Alban's Head, which may have originally commemorated the first Romano-British martyr, who came from the town in Hertfordshire that carries his name.

Worth Matravers

Square and Compass ① 🚌
Renscombe Farm ■ ⑫ ⑬ ✝
⑨ ⑭ ②
⑩ ③
⑪ Weston Seacombe
✗ Royal Marines Farm Bottom
memorial East ④
man's Man Seacombe
ool Emmetts ⑦
Hill ⑤
St Aldhelm's Quarry Winspit
⑧ The
Plain
Pier Bottom ✝
⑥
St Alban's Head

⊢ 500 m ⊣

Square and Compass

1 Set off downhill (S) to the **Square and Compass** in 150 metres. Turn left (NE) at the junction and pass the 1808-dated former **Wesleyan Chapel**. Turn right at the gate and stile immediately before the three **Abbascombe** houses in 200 metres. Enter National Trust land and follow the stone wall around to the left (S) in 25 metres, seawards along a former cultivation terrace into the pastures of **East Man** hillside. Turn left (E) through the wall, over a stone stile, in 300 metres.

2 Begin by following a another lynchet and cross two fields. Re-enter National Trust land midway along the lower side of the hedge in 300 metres.

3 Turn right here (SE) to enter **Seacombe Bottom**. Turn right (S) on joining the main track in 300 metres. Our onward route is on the right in 500 metres but if you have the energy and time, continue along the valley path to pass underground gallery quarries and look down on the ledges of **Seacombe Cliff**.

4 Having started to climb out of the valley (SW) the sea is now to our left. In 500 metres, on passing through a gap in blackthorn scrub, the coast path is above the

Seacombe quarries

Halsewell Rock where 82 survivors of the stricken East Indiaman clung for their lives and were rescued by quarrymen in 1786. In a further 750 metres the path descends into **Winspit Bottom** where former quarries to the left include a bat refuge.

 Turn right on reaching the valley floor and then turn left,

in just 15 metres, to follow the fence uphill. Keep to the trodden path as there is a precipitous drop from unfenced slope to the left. It is safer to slip on the mud than slide on the grass. The coast path then passes above a ribbon of limestone cliffs with breeding peregrine falcons and ravens to the National Coastwatch lookout on **St Alban's Head** in 2,000 metres.

The Telecommunications Research Establishment at Renscombe Farm was the top-secret wartime base for electronic boffins who developed advanced radar equipment and devised counter-measures to thwart German wireless-directed bombing beams.

 Turn right (NE) along the untarred road between Norman **St Aldhelm's Chapel** and Victorian **Coastguard Cottages** along the track across featureless fields known as **The Plain**. Pass Trevor Haysom's **St Aldhelm's Quarry** in 900 metres.

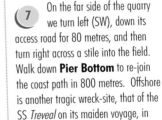 On the far side of the quarry we turn left (SW), down its access road for 80 metres, and then turn right across a stile into the field. Walk down **Pier Bottom** to re-join the coast path in 800 metres. Offshore is another tragic wreck-site, that of the SS *Treveal* on its maiden voyage, in 1922.

 Turn right (N), up steps from near sea level to the 400-feet plateau of **Emmetts Hill**, which means 'Anthill' in the Dorset dialect. In 1,000 metres, overlooking Chapman's Pool, the path passes the memorial to the 20th-century war dead of the Royal Marines. Continue from it along the cliff path for a further 500 metres.

 Turn right (NE) over a stile beside a hunting gate and

Underground cliff quarries at Seacombe and Winspit, with galleries up to 12 feet high, were last worked in the Second World War and are now refuges for Britain's rarest bats.

walk straight ahead across the first field, and a little leftward through the second field, to a car-park to the right of **Renscombe Farm** in 600 metres.

Eastern Winspit

10 Cross the corner of the car-park and then its access track to a stile immediately opposite the entrance. The path (E) crosses the site of the top-secret wartime **Telecommunications Research Establishment** to **Weston Farm** in 400 metres.

(11) Turn left beside the farmyard, up the track, and then right along the road in 50 metres.

(12) Turn left (N) on reaching Worth Matravers village, in 400 metres, immediately after the driveways to **Westmanton** and **Bladon**. A public path into the children's play area follows the ivy-clad wall up the slope to a stile in 75 metres. Pass to the left of the stone wall beside Bladon and continue straight ahead to the end of the paddock in 50 metres.

(13) Here a second path turns right (W) into the field behind the churchyard. Turn right across the stile at the end of hedge in 100 metres. Go through the gate in

Headland seamark

the next corner (S), in 15 metres, and down for 100 metres, via **St Nicholas Church** with a fine Norman chancel arch, to the street.

(14) Turn left (E) beside the village green and pond to pass the **Post Office** and return to the junction beside the **Square and Compass** in 250 metres. Here we turn left (N) to return to the car-park in 250 metres.

Mesozoic sauropod footprints discovered by Worth Matravers quarryman Kevin Keates in 1997 - since safely sealed again underground - are the biggest set of multiple dinosaur tracks ever found in the British Isles.

Royal Marines memorial

8 Durlston Head & Dancing Ledge

Quarries throughout in a 6-mile circuit round-walk across big tracts of conservation land

Unwanted pieces of Victorian London abound on and around Durlston Head, being brought back from the capital by stone merchant George Burt who succeeded contractor John Mowlem as an entrepreneur and developer. Thomas Hardy called him 'the King of Swanage'. Burt bought Durlston Head in 1864 and built its palatial Riviera-style mock castle in 1886-87. Its inspired speciality feature is the Great Globe, which is surrounded by innumerable inscriptions, to bring science and knowledge to the visitor. Researching the origin of the stones becomes a study in itself. 'Durlston Head Castle, above sea 215 feet', for instance, is on a granite pillar ordered by Sir Charles Barry for Trafalgar Square. The octagonal portals to former quarries at Tilly Whim

Level:
Length: 6 miles
Terrain: Well-marked paths almost entirely across access land with only minor slopes.
Park and start: Follow brown signs through **Swanage**, via the Seymer Road, Durlston Road and Lighthouse Road to the car-park for **Durlston Country Park**.
Start ref: SZ 033 773.
Postcode: BH19 2JN
Public transport: Summertime buses through Swanage.
Websites: www.durlston.co.uk
www.swanagerailway.co.uk

Caves used to form the entrance to Pentonville Prison. Durlston Country Park, created by county planning officer Alan Swindall, opened in 1974.

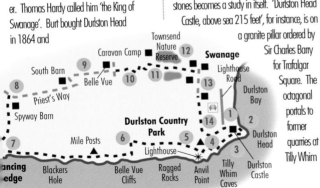

Durlston Castle

1. Set off down the slope (SE) from the marker for 243 feet above sea level to **Durlston Castle Bar and Restaurant** in 150 metres. Entrance columns to Victorian contractor George Burt's seaside villa give its original 'Durlston Head Castle' name (and tell us we are now at 215 feet above the English Channel).

2. Bear left down beside the outer wall, along **Round the Head**, as the path is called. The seawards view is to the Needles of the Isle of Wight. Across to the left is what becomes a perfect view of Durlston Bay, Peveril Point, Ballard Down and vertical slabs on Bournemouth's skyline. At the corner, in 225 metres, we are on **Durlston Head** (at 111 feet above the sea). Proceed a further

80 metres and go up steps, for 50 metres, to admire the 40-ton, 10-feet diameter **Great Globe**. It takes half an hour to digest words of science, scripture and wisdom in a multitude of inscriptions.

3. Return down the steps for 50 metres and turn right (SW) along the coast path. Pass a viewing point in 150 metres. Downwards is for dolphins (the best indicator is a cloud of gulls circling over a school).

Next along the cliffs we pass the 1887-dated former entrance pillar from Pentonville Prison at the entrance to underground quarries at **Tilly Whim Caves** which have been closed since regular rockfalls began in 1976.

4 Take the over-ground option and then weave down and across valley below **Mile Post** masts (marking a nautical mile) to arise in 250 metres on the seaward side of **Anvil Point Lighthouse**.

5 Turn right (NW), to head inland on its access road, but only for 200 metres. Then turn left through the scrub to a kissing gate in the stone wall. Proceed up the slope on to **Round Down** and go through

a similar gate (W) in the next wall in 200 metres. Cross the earthworks of an early 19th-century semaphore station, in 50 metres, and even more undulating quarry workings for the following 300 metres. We are on the coastal ridge above Ragged Rocks and disused Half Moon Quarry. Cross the boundary wall of the country park at the end of the next orchid-rich pasture in another 300 metres.

> Work started on Anvil Point Lighthouse in 1880 and it was operational two years later, though not in time to save the Liverpool sailing ship Alexandrovna which was dashed to pieces on the rocks below, on 29 April 1882.

Tilly Whim

6 Turn left (S) on the other side, down to the National Trust's **Belle Vue Cliffs**, in 175 metres. Turn right (W) and follow the clifftop path, above inaccessible **Blackers Hole** in 1,500 metres, to accessible **Dancing Ledge** in a further 1,000 metres.

7 Turn right (NE) from the entry point to the quarry shelf, up the right-hand slope, for 300 metres. Go through the wall and follow the well-marked path straight ahead (N) across the plateau to **Spyway Barn** in 600 metres. Continue from this National Trust farmyard across grassland beyond to the **Priest's Way** in 150 metres. This takes its name from Worth Matravers clergy having to travel to Swanage to conduct services there.

8 Turn right (E) and follow the stony green lane to the next tract of open grassland around **South Barn** in 1,000 metres. Here the historic route continues straight ahead as an overgrown depression, from which the present right of way strikes off sharply to the left, passing the corner of South Barn and following its drive (N) away from the house. Cross the cattle-grid and turn right (E) along the next section of the Priest's Way.

9 Keep going straight ahead, across a stone stile, at the next corner. Cross a pasture as you approach the next cluster of buildings, **Belle Vue Farm**, in 800 metres. Leave the main track at the cross-roads of paths, straight ahead beside the sheds of an underground stone mine. Keep this to your right and cross two fields into caravan country in 400 metres.

Anvil Point Lighthouse

10 Turn left in the scrubby corner to enter the **Caravan Park**. Proceed for only 4 metres. Then turn right across a second stile in the gap in the hedge. Turn right (SE) on the other side and down the drive through the caravans to a cross-roads in 100 metres. Turn left (N), beneath the lamp standard, downhill for 150 metres. Turn right (E) at the sycamore tree in the oval of grass. Head uphill to the next triangle of grass in 100 metres. Turn left and keep bearing right - down and round the bend - to climb to the top end of the path (between mobile homes 179 and 179A) in 150 metres.

11 Here we exit from the caravans, cross a road, and enter Dorset Wildlife Trust's **Townsend Nature Reserve** across the remains of quarry shafts and spoil heaps. Continue straight ahead, following the fence for 150 metres, and then along a stony track for 100 metres. Also proceed straight ahead at the cross-roads of tracks beside two crabstones which held the mule-drawn capstan for operating the steep slide down a ferny shaft which is now a bat refuge.

12 Bear left and then go straight ahead at the next series of path crossings to follow waymarks and a fence to the end of industrial archaeology wilderness zone in 300 metres. Cross the road into the public footpath opposite. This cuts through more bramble and blackthorn scrub on **Rough Heights** and passes the 1954-dated **Old Barn** in 200 metres.

13 In 75 metres we come to **Russell Avenue**. Cross into **Russell Drive** (S) which goes down into the valley at **South Barn** in 500 metres. Continue straight ahead along the path for a further 500 metres, up and over the hill, into **Durlston Country Park**.

14 Turn left (E), at the top of the coastal slope, down to the road from the lighthouse in 150 metres. Turn left to return to the car-park in a further 150 metres.

Dancing Ledge

9 Ulwell & Godlingston

A 5-mile National Trust circuit of the barrow-studded central massif of the Purbeck Hills

Explore inland Purbeck, beside and then along the hog's back of its chalk spine, midway between Corfe Castle and Studland. Most of the hill country access land is in National Trust ownership. The views present an extensive panorama around the entirety of Poole Harbour and across Poole Bay to the next piece of matching chalkland - which was continuous until the sea broke through after the last Ice Age - at the Needles of the Isle of Wight. Chalkland flora is well represented, together with butterflies when the microclimate performs, on sheltered south-facing slopes along the main escarpment. Straddling the top it is an ancient barrow-studded landscape with a strip of common land which has remained open and unenclosed.

Level:
Length: 5 miles
Terrain: Good going throughout with the only real climb, on to the Purbeck Hills, being its gentlest possible ascent.
Park and start: In the large layby at **Ulwell** with the 'Welcome to Swanage' sign between **Filberts Meadow** and **Shepherds Farm**.
Start ref: SZ 021 809.
Postcode: BH19 3DG
Public transport: Buses between Swanage, Studland and Bournemouth.
Websites: www.langtonia.org.uk
www.visitswanageandpurbeck.co.uk

Map:

combe
ll

Ailwood Down
8
Purbeck Hills
7
Kingswood Down
⁂
Nine Barrow Down
9
Godlingston Down
masts ▲
Godlingston Hill
Obelisk
Ballard Down
11
12 🚗
Shepherds Farm ■
6
Knitson Farm ■
Godlingston Manor ■
10
1
5
4
2 **Ulwell**
3
from Swanage
↑ North
Windmill Knap
Tom Burnham's Oak
Ulwell Village Inn

500 m

Godlingston Manor, one of the oldest inhabited buildings in Dorset, incorporates a fortified tower refuge with walls 5-feet thick, which dates from about 1300.

 Set off towards Swanage (SE), to the junction in 100 metres, and turn right (SW) beside **Bramble Cottage** to pass **Ulwell Cottage Caravans** and **Ulwell Village Inn** to the corner in 150 metres. Continue straight ahead from here (ignoring a second path signed to the right) and follow the hedge of **Bear Cottage** with caravans up the slope to your right. Also continue straight ahead into the field beyond, in 125 metres, with

Swanage to the left and the Purbeck Hills to the right.

Proceed from the end of the pasture in 250 metres, following the hedge towards the wood, to a path junction in 200 metres. Turn left - downhill towards Herston - and then bear right with a lake up to your right.

Turn right (W) on reaching the farm track in 300 metres. Pass historic **Godlingston Manor** and go through the farmyard. Follow the hedge straight ahead and then keep **Marsh Copse** to your left, to the road in 600 metres.

Turn left (S), with caravans to the right, uphill to the corner

Godlingston Manor

in 150 metres. Turn right (W) into the leafy green lane beside **Tom Burnham's Oak**. Continue beside oak trees on the hillside beyond, beside **Windmill Knap**, to the end of the long arable field in 500 metres.

(5) Turn right (N), down into the valley, and then uphill through **Knitson Farm** in 600 metres. Turn left at the road, following it around the bend, to **Dairy Cottage** and the next corner, in 50 metres. Turn right here, up the drive

of **Knitson Old Farmhouse**, and proceed to the foot of the escarpment in 175 metres.

(6) Turn left (NW), beside the chalk and gravel pit, and go through the gate in 75 metres. Bear

Tom Burnham's Oak is named for a suicide burial, which were traditionally at what was then a cross-roads on the parish boundary, with a stake through the heart to lay the ghost.

Knitson Farm

left (W) to follow the hedgerow, with fields to the left and the chalk escarpment rising to the right. Go through a bridleway gate into National Trust land in 400 metres and take the upper fork along a well-trod terrace.

(7) Then in 900 metres we rise to a gate. Continue along this lower path for a further 300 metres and then bear right (NW) up the chalky track on to the spine of the

Purbeck Hills in another 300 metres.

(8) Turn right (SE) on the summit, following the fence uphill along **Brenscombe Hill** pasture and re-enter National Trust access land on **Ailwood Down** in 300 metres. Follow the hilltop track for

300 metres and then fork left to pass the line of prehistoric burial mounds on **Nine Barrow Down** in another 300 metres. They offer a panoramic view over Poole Harbour.

(9) Head for the masts and then bear to the right to rejoin the main track and go through the gate in

A tower windmill on Windmill Knap, which remained as a ruin into the 19th century, is said to have been built with stone from a mediaeval ranger's lodge which was still standing in 1618.

800 metres. Continue straight ahead for 1,000 metres and then with the masts up to the left follow the farm track as it drops (SE) towards Swanage Bay and enters National Trust downland in 200 metres.

(10) Descend (E) through the hollow between **Godlingston Hill** and **Round Down**, for 1,000 metres, to approach the road from

Ailwood Down

Studland to Swanage. Then bear left (NE), for 150 metres, to the left-hand roadside gate.

(11) Turn left (N), to the junction in 20 metres, and then right (E) into more National Trust land on the other side of the **Ulwell Gap**. Having gone through the gate, proceed for just 20 metres, and then turn right (SE) to follow the terrace at the foot of the escarpment. Go through the kissing gate in 350 metres which comprises four ex-City of London cannon bollards.

(12) Bear right in 25 metres (S), downhill beside a granite inscription commemorating the Swanage Water Act of 1883, to return to the layby through another cannon-bollarded gate in 100 metres.

Swanage view

10 Ower & Studland

An 11-mile exploration of Purbeck's twin coasts with heath, forest and sand dunes

Level: 🥾 🥾
Length: 11 miles
Terrain: On the wild side but with well-marked paths and no demanding climb.
Park and start: In the viewpoint layby between **Kingswood Farm** and **Purbeck Golf Course** and Kingswood, beside the B3351, from Corfe Castle to Studland.
Start ref: SZ 006 818.
Postcode: BH20 5JQ
Public transport: Buses from Studland to Swanage.
Websites: www.isleofpurbeck.com
www.nationaltrust.org.uk

Though covered with post-war Forestry Commission conifers at Rempstone, an immense expanse of Dorset's original heathland habitat flourishes from there to the sea at Studland. Heather-clad knolls are interspersed with wide bogs enlivened by cotton grass and the stunning blue flowers of marsh gentians. Sand lizards and their rare smooth snake predators move underfoot. Sika and roe deer share the forest and the heath. The green woodpecker functions as an audio barometer with its 'yaffle' cry giving it the reputation as Dorset's rain-bird. Heron and great-crested grebe fish Little Sea lagoon, beyond which a sand dune system unfolds to reveal a nudist beach beside the grade-one honeypot of Dorset's holiday coast. Beaches, downs and heaths in Studland parish were bequeathed to the National Trust by landowner Ralph Bankes of Kingston Lacy House in 1981.

Map labels:
Newton Bay
5
6 Newton
Greenland Farm 7
Bird hide
Little Sea
8
Rempstone Forest
3
Studland Heath
9
Knoll Beach
Knoll House Hotel
Godlingston Heath
Agglestone Rock ▲
14
10 Middle Beach
Wadmore
South Beach
11
2
Golf Course
17
15
13 12
Fishing Barrow ☀
1
Studland
Bankes Arms
16
B3351 from Corfe Castle
Club House
500 m

Rempstone Forest

(1) Set off across the stile at the centre of the layby down into the pasture (NW). Cross into the arable field in 100 metres, diagonally to the left-hand corner, in 200 metres. Go through the gate and keep the fence to your left for 400 metres. Bear right as you approach the corner of woodland, on to a second path, 100 metres to the right of these trees and the power lines. The gorse of a hedgerow is now to your right. This leads down to a bridge at **Foxground** in a further 400 metres.

(2) Proceed straight ahead (N). Cross the woodland track in 350 metres, into a lesser track, for 200 metres. Turn right on reaching the next sandy ride to head through the central plantings of **Purbeck** **Forest** across the former **Newton Heath**.

(3) On joining the next gravel road, in 900 metres, we turn left (NW) and then cross a tarred oil-field road. Continue straight ahead along the gravel road on the other side. In 800 metres the track becomes deep off-white sand on leaving the pine forest. Proceed straight ahead to a cross-roads of tracks in 150 metres.

(4) Here we have a diversion, straight ahead, to **Ower**